RESENTMENTS

and

FORGIVENESS

Wayne Kauppila

DISCLAIMER: *Any form of therapy or counseling has inherent associated risks. The Forgiveness Therapy method put forth in this book has these risks. The author makes no claim, either stated or implied, that forgiveness therapy is without risk. Therefore, it is the reader's responsibility to ensure their safety before practicing the methods presented in this book. Because therapy is highly subjective, the author also makes no guarantee as to the effectiveness of Forgiveness Therapy.*

RESENTMENTS
and
FORGIVENESS

This book was written to help you heal your resentments. It provides a simple straightforward set of steps which when followed have helped thousands of people achieve freedom from their resentments using forgiveness therapy. You may be thinking, "I have already forgiven those who have hurt me." In many cases, this thought is simply a defense mechanism that is protecting deeply buried emotions. If you can, set aside these thoughts and take an honest look at what might be hiding underneath. This book will help you do that.

SAFETY FIRST

Reading this book has risks. A few people who started the process outlined in this book have become suicidal. This happens because they uncover long buried feelings of worthlessness, hopelessness and helplessness. These are the suicide emotions. If you decide to read on, make an agreement with someone you trust like a family member, friend or therapist that you will seek out help should you start to feel like killing yourself. If you become suicidal, you can call the National Suicide Prevention Lifeline at 1-800-273-8255.

Another safety factor to consider is dissociation. Some people, when presented with the information about different types of abuse, have dissociated. Dissociation happens when your focus and awareness are totally absorbed in some traumatic experience from your past and you lose touch with the here and now. Reading this book may re-traumatize you and you will need skills to keep part of your awareness in the here and now. Or else, you may need professional help if you dissociate. The skill required to stay in the here and now is called "grounding." Listed below are some grounding skills you may use when reading. For others, you will need to stop reading and focus on grounding until your awareness is back in the present moment.

GROUNDING SKILLS TO USE WHILE READING:

✓ Use a highlighter or pen and underline or highlight sentences that have meaning to you.

✓ Doodle in the margins.

✓ Curl and uncurl your toes.

✓ Clench and unclench your fists.

✓ Roll some keys, a koosh ball, a stress ball, etc. around in your hand.

✓ Push your feet down and wiggle your toes.

✓ Tighten you butt muscles and relax them. Repeat this over and over.

✓ Squeeze your kneecaps.

✓ Hold an ice cube in one hand.

✓ Smoke a cigarette while reading.

✓ Focus on your breathing.

✓ Pray and ask your higher power to help you through this.

✓ Ask your higher power for the power to heal. (The last part of Step 11)

✓ Ask your higher power for willingness.

Combine several of the above to stay present.

Skills to use for more severe forms of dissociation.

✓ Lay on your back on the ground with your palms facing down. (Literally grounding yourself) While doing this, breathe with belly muscles, not your chest muscles. Think of something positive and repeat a short phrase in your head. For example, "I will get through this and heal." "My mother loves me" "God loves me."

✓ Have a friend push your feet into the floor.

✓ Listen to your favorite music.

✓ Take a shower or a bath.

✓ Go for a walk.

✓ If after trying these grounding skills you are still getting stuck in your traumas, seek professional help. A therapist can help you reduce the intensity of your feelings.

HOPE

There is hope. Thousands of people have used Forgiveness therapy to heal their resentments. The following story is an example of hope and healing

Hope for Frankie and His Family

In the month of July, on Frankie's 8th birthday, his uncle took him into a locked bedroom and sodomized him. Frankie never talked about it and buried the emotions deep inside. He grew up, got married and had a family of his own. He was a model citizen; he had a good job and a nice house. But every July Frankie would change into a monster. Every July without fail, he would get a domestic violence charge. Frankie had been through all of the mental health services available in his area. He had talked to many counselors and therapists, but the problem remained. Every July he would beat up his wife. Frankie was referred for Forgiveness Therapy. The first session was his assessment where he talked openly about what his uncle did to him. In his second session, he identified all the resentments he felt about the situation, and he composed a prayer of forgiveness exactly like the one found further along in this book. He was given directions to repeat his prayer twice daily. In his third and final session, several weeks later, Frankie took the forgiveness test and passed. That was the end of his therapy. A year passed and one-day Frankie's wife came in the office to say thank-you. She told the story how July had come and gone, and how Frankie had not acted out and hurt her. She expressed her gratitude for the help that Frankie had received which had helped him finally heal those old wounds.

The Doctor's Wife

The doctor's wife was sick. She was always getting sick. She was in the emergency room two or three times a month complaining of vomiting and diarrhea. The doctors could never figure out a medical reason for her sickness, because none existed. She was exhibiting "psycho-somatic" symptoms. Her sickness started out psychologically and then moved into the body- showing up as physical illness.

The doctor's wife had been sexually molested by her grandfather when she young. Repeatedly he would come to her room and molest her. She was young and defenseless against this abuse. One day her intuition told her that he was about to do it again, and she started throwing up. Her grandfather did not molest her that day because she was sick. Unconsciously she was forming a very effective defense mechanism. She began to get sick more and more so that she could protect herself from him. Eventually she grew up, got married to the doctor and had children. Life is stressful and unconsciously she would become sick to cope with her anxiety.

The doctor's wife was given the author's book *Opening the Door to Freedom with Forgiveness Therapy*. She did the work all on her own without any help from a counselor or therapist. She was able to heal herself with forgiveness. Her somatic symptoms completely disappeared. She no longer needed the defense mechanism she created to protect herself against the resentments she had held onto for so long. She did the work outlined in this book and freed herself. There is hope for you. You can heal yourself just like she did, and you can be free of resentments.

WHAT IS RESENTMENT?

Resentment is re-feeling something from your past.

For example, A mother starts telling her son from an early age "you were a mistake," "I don't love you," "I should have had an abortion when I found out I was pregnant with you." This young boy feels worthless, unloved and unprotected. As the boy grows, his mother's actions continue to show him that she really doesn't love him. Her other children are shown love and support, but he is left out. The boy begins to feel increasingly more hopeless and helpless because his mother isn't changing. The boy carries these resentments with him as he matures into a young man. He keeps feeling worthless, rejected, unloved. His hopelessness and helplessness grow stronger and stronger. He begins to use alcohol to drown these feelings. This temporary solution starts to ruin his young life. He loses his job, and then his house, and then his friends and family. Soon he is living in his car, alone and afraid. His outside world begins to match his inside world. He decides that he is going to kill himself. Prepared with two bottles of pills and a fifth of whiskey, he is ready to die. He decides to call his brother to say goodbye. That call saved his life. His brother took his suicidal intentions seriously and offered to pay for him to get into a treatment center. The young man accepted the help.

Within the safe space of the treatment center, he is no longer in danger of harming himself. He has the opportunity to safely examine his past and all of the resentments that were driving him to kill himself. He was killing himself slowly with alcohol and when that didn't work, he decided he was going to speed up the process with suicide. What he was really trying to kill were his resentments, those feelings of worthlessness, hopelessness and helplessness. Whether you are reading this book in treatment, or on your own, you can learn how to let go of resentments so they no longer drive you or your addiction.

The Big book of Alcoholics Anonymous says on page 64 "Resentment is the number one offender. It destroys more alcoholics than anything else." Why is this true? Think of your addiction as a car and think of your resentments as the gas that fuels the car.

This gas or resentment can kill you in two ways: first, it fuels your addiction and the addiction kills you, or secondly, the gas itself will kill you because it contains the suicide emotions of worthlessness, hopelessness, and helplessness. This book will show you a way to empty that gas tank of resentments.

WHAT IS FORGIVENESS?

If resentments are hanging on to old feelings, then forgiveness is letting them go. The question is, how do I forgive? The answer is found by reading the rest of this book and doing the suggested work. The forgiveness process outlined in this book is simple:

1. Begin by reading the following pages to learn about where resentments come from and put a check in the box by the ones you have experienced, or use a highlighter to identify abuse use have suffered. This is difficult work so please don't deny the reality of what happened to you.

2. Now go back through your checks and highlighted areas with a feeling list found further on in this book. Circle the feelings you have for one person. Only do one person at a time. Use a separate feelings list for each person.

3. Narrow down the circled feelings to the 10 that bother you the most and put a star next to those feelings.

4. Now you will use the starred feelings to create a forgiveness prayer. The smaller resentments will automatically be healed because forgiveness is generalizable.

5. Now use the prayer format in the back of this book and fill it in with the name of the appropriate person and the feelings and resentments you have starred for them.

6. Repeat the prayer at least twice a day out loud. Repeat it more if you want to heal faster.

7. You are ready to take the forgiveness test when you feel like you are done.

WHERE DO RESENTMENTS COME FROM?

The following pages contain many examples of where resentments can be generated. As you read the examples, put a check in the box if the example happened to you. If the example reminds you of something similar that happened to you, write it in the space provided below each example.

Denial of Reality

❑ Denial of reality is a form of abuse that can be difficult to understand. This form of abuse happens when a parent or a caregiver tells a child that some form of abuse didn't happen, or that it wasn't that bad.

_____

_____

_____

_____

_____

❑ A single mother of an 8 year old girl lives in poverty with her child. By some stroke of luck she meets and marries a wealthy cardiologist. Both the mother's and the daughter's lifestyles change dramatically. The mother now has money to go places she has never been and buy things she could never afford. The mother gets her sister to start babysitting her daughter so she can go out. The eight year old little girl ends up getting raped by her uncle. When the little girl tells her mother what happened the mom doesn't believe her and states "That didn't happen to you, and don't tell your dad about any of that nonsense, I am not going to lose this big house!" The mother has denied the little girl's reality. Consequently, the raping continues for three years and the mother's response to her daughter is essentially the same; "Those things aren't happening, your making it all up. Don't you dare tell your dad." The little girl turns into a young woman and ends up spending most of her teen years in psyche hospitals, until she escapes and lives on the street. On the street she turns to a life of prostitution and drug use. She gives birth to three babies and they are all taken away by the state. She was about to lose a fourth baby to the state when she decided to get help. When she started to identify her resentments, she found that her biggest one was for her mother.

_____

_____

_____

_____

_____

_____

☐ A young boy gets beat on his bare butt with a belt by his mother. As he grows older he becomes full of anger and rage. As an adult, he starts therapy to deal with his negative emotions. He confronts his mother with the memories of her hitting him with the belt when he was a child. The mother responds coldly, "That never happened, and shame on you for bringing it up and disgracing the family."

_____

_____

_____

_____

_____

☐ As you continue to read this book, don't deny your own reality. As you read about the different forms of abuse, be honest with yourself and put a check mark in the box beside the abuse issues that have happened to you. To thy own self be true. Without honesty you will never get better. Being honest with yourself is a spiritual experience. The good news is that with help you can heal these resentments. You can then experience inner peace, freedom and lightness.

If you become overwhelmed while reading, put this book down and take a break. Spend some time processing your emotions in a healthy manner. And when you feel courageous again, continue reading and doing the work.

Your Secrets Will Keep You Sick

❑ If you were abused and lived in an environment where you were not allowed to talk about the abuse and that was the unspoken rule, then you experienced denial of reality in an unspoken form. When children cannot speak up to stop abuse from happening, when they cannot scream out in anger or pain, they suffer silently. Feelings get denied and this emotional energy gets buried deep inside them, and these secrets will keep them sick.

_____

_____

_____

_____

_____

Physical Abuse

There are two categories of physical abuse; overt and covert.

❑ Overt physical abuse is when your body is hurt. Examples include: punching, kicking, slapping, being thrown to the ground, breaking bones, being hit with an object like a frying pan, a switch, a board, being hit by a car, being thrown from a car, being choked, strangled or restrained with anything, being shot or stabbed, being pinched. In some cases even tickling can be abuse.

_____

_____

_____

_____

_____

What about spankings?

☐ When a child is spanked they naturally have a lot of negative feelings. Spanking is an example of negative re-enforcement. The spanking teaches the child to obey the rules. But what about the feelings? Were they too much for the situation? Did that anger and that rage get buried behind walls. Does the spanking start to form resentments that are protected by thoughts like "everyone gets a spanking." "If they didn't love me they wouldn't spank me."

_____

_____

_____

_____

_____

Remember you are doing this work to identify your resentments. So don't deny your feelings about being spanked. The following example will help you differentiate between discipline, which we all need, and abuse, which can generate resentments.

☐ Little Johnny is five years old and his mother has established clear rules that he cannot eat cookies before dinner. Johnny breaks the rule and eats a cookie. He gets caught of course, and mom reminds him of the rule and then spanks his bottom with an open hand. Johnny cries a little and that is it. Mom set clear rules and when the rule was broken, she disciplined her child. This whole scenario was affirming to Johnny learning how to function in society.

_____

_____

_____

_____

_____

❑ Same scenario on a different day, only on this day Johnny's dad is at the bar drinking up the rent money and mom is freaking out because they will be evicted if the rent is not paid. Again, Johnny breaks mom's rule and eats cookies before dinner. Again, mom catches him. She gets a large wooden spoon, pulls his pants down, bends him over her knees and whacks his bare butt several times with the wooden spoon, leaving marks. This has crossed the line from discipline to abuse. It is no longer helping Johnny learn discipline, it is helping him to build resentments.

_____

_____

_____

_____

_____

❑ So to help you figure out of your spankings were abusive or not, ask yourself this question: Were they affirming? Did they help me to learn self discipline or do I have a resentment? Was is abusive? It can be very difficult to admit that you were abused by a parent.

_____

_____

_____

_____

_____

❑ Admitting you were abused by your parent is doubly hard because you have to get over two big obstacles. The first is to give up your childish ideas that your parents are perfect. We have all these this ideas because when we are children, our higher powers are our parents and we believe they are perfect. So take them off the pedestal. Your parents aren't perfect. Second, and just as difficult is to admit that they abused me as well. A true double whammy!

_____

_____

_____

_____

_____

Covert Physical Abuse

☐ Covert physical abuse is when you didn't get enough of something. Examples include; not having a safe place to live, not having appropriate clothes for the weather, like having a hole in your sneaker and walking through snow to school, not having enough food, or good food to eat, not having heat or air conditioning in the house, not having running water at all, not feeling safe when sleeping, living in a house where fear is pervasive, such as domestic violence, fights, raging.

_____

_____

_____

_____

_____

The Boy in the Car

Sam was 16 and in treatment for using any kind of drug, he could get his hands on. His mother called and said that she would like to stop in and visit. When Sam was told this news, he was not happy and became very emotional. He tried very hard to convince his therapist that his mom should not visit. He even ratted her out on her drug use, which he knew was running the risk of child protective services being involved in his case. His mom did show up to visit and it was obvious from her dirty hair and clothes that she was most likely homeless.

Throughout the meeting with his mom, Sam hung his head in shame. He did not want anyone to know how worthless he felt about the true story. Sam and his mother had been living in their car for many years. After his mother left, Sam spilled his guts about his life with his mother in the car. Throughout his story telling, the strength of Sam's love for his mother was evident. He was also very protective of her.

It was very hard work for Sam to admit that his living situation was covertly abusive, but he did and after he forgave his mom for his resentment of unworthiness, he uncovered a great motivation to remain clean and sober. He started talking with great joy about his plan to become successful so that he could buy his mother a house to live in.

I Want to Stay in Jail

A 19-year-old, Native American, female is in drug court and only has a few months to go before her graduation. She attends a cultural celebration on her reservation and afterwards a group of her friends invites her to party with them. She goes to the party and drinks violating the drug court rules. She goes on the run and is picked up on a warrant a few weeks later. Now in jail, she is asked if she wants to get out and do drug court again. "No, I want to stay in jail," she says. When she is asked why, she responds, "The house I live in has no running water, and the furnace is broken so it is very cold. Most days there is nothing in the house to eat. My mom is always bringing different guys home and they are always drunk or high. They try to have sex with me. I want to stay in jail because it is safe here. I can talk to sober people. I can take a hot shower. I get regular meals to eat."

This young woman was experiencing many forms of *covert physical abuse*. So much in fact, that jail was a better place to live than home with her mother.

Did you get enough hugs?

❑ Another form of covert physical abuse is not getting enough loving physical touch. An extreme example of this was revealed in Hitler's plans to breed super soldiers. Hitler had breeding facilities to create a white Arian soldier who would kill without having any feelings. In these facilities, tall, blonde haired, blue-eyed men would mate with tall, blonde haired blue-eyed women to produce babies with the exact same features. The male babies would be given the best medical attention and food, but the nurses were not allowed to touch the babies. Neither one of the parents were allowed to touch the babies either. These babies had no physical contact with another human and the results were disastrous. All the babies died. They did not get to nurse at their mother's breasts. They did not get cuddled or hugged. Did you?

_____

_____

_____

_____

_____

RAD: Reactive Attachment Disorder

☐ Reactive attachment disorder is caused when a child does not receive enough loving attention from their parents or caregivers. This is seen in the many adopted children from Russia. The Russian orphanages are overcrowded and understaffed so the children are not getting enough loving attention from their caregivers. Children of addicts and alcoholics can also suffer from RAD because the parents are spending all their time getting high, or recovering from being dope sick, or they are out looking for more drugs. RAD manifests with the symptom of not being able to make meaningful human connections, which is a lack of empathy.

_____

_____

_____

_____

_____

Sexual Abuse

There are two general categories of sexual abuse, overt and covert.

❑ Overt sexual abuse is when something is done to your body or you are forced to do something sexual to someone else. Examples include: vaginal or anal rape, rape with a finger or an object, inappropriate touching or kissing, sexual bondage or torture. Being forced to masturbate someone or being forced to give oral sex to someone. Incest is having sex with a family member.

_____

_____

_____

_____

_____

❑ Covert sexual abuse is when you have uncomfortable feelings but nothing is physically done to your body. Examples include: being exposed to sexual information like pornography at an early age, watching your parents have sex, knowing that mom or dad is having an affair, watching someone sexually molest your brother or sister and not being able to stop it, or worse helping it to happen.

_____

_____

_____

_____

_____

❑ The boyfriend was bad.

Mom would bring her two young boys to be babysat by her older daughter's boyfriend. When he was alone in the house with the two young boys, the boyfriend would sexually molest one of the young boys while his brother was forced to hold a blanket over the window so no one could see in. The boyfriend would finish with one boy and the brothers would switch places. One of these boys came into treatment and he was able to forgive the boyfriend for molesting him, but he had the most difficult time forgiving himself for holding the blanket over the window while his brother was being molested. By the way, the boyfriend is now spending a long time in prison. This young man experienced both forms of sexual abuse. Overt sexual abuse was done to him and covert sexual abuse happened when he held the blanket over the window while his brother was being raped. In this case, the covert abuse was worse than the overt abuse.

_____

_____

_____

_____

_____

_____

_____

_____

☐ Jokes or inappropriate comments about a person's sexuality are also forms of covert sexual abuse.

_____

_____

_____

_____

_____

_____

☐ Being called names like whore, slut, trifling ho and the "c" word are forms of covert sexual abuse.

_____

_____

_____

_____

_____

_____

☐ Derogatory comments about breast size or penis size are forms of covert sexual abuse.

_____

_____

_____

_____

_____

_____

☐ Comments like "you will go blind" or "you will grow hair on your palms" are forms of covert sexual abuse.

_____

_____

_____

_____

_____

_____

☐ Not getting truthful sexual education or being taught fear or shame regarding sex is covert sexual abuse.

_____

_____

_____

_____

_____

_____

_____

☐ Being rejected for your sexual orientation is a form of covert sexual abuse.

_____

_____

_____

_____

_____

_____

☐ Being told that masturbation is a sin is covert sexual abuse.

_____

_____

_____

_____

_____

_____

Mental Abuse

❏ Mental abuse happens when logical thinking is not supported or encouraged. An example seen most often is a when a child brings home a good report card and no one gives the child kudos or affirmations for getting good grades. The child starts to think that there is no point in trying and begins to feel hopeless.

_____

_____

_____

_____

_____

_____

_____

❏ Another example of mental abuse is not being taught healthy problem solving skills. For example, Dad comes home from work complaining of a stressful day. He fixes a double martini to cope with his stress. The problem solving skill he has just taught his children is; "When you are stressed out you drink alcohol." Marijuana or other drugs can also be used in this scenario.

_____

_____

_____

_____

_____

_____

☐ An extreme form of mental abuse was discovered in a five-year-old boy who still could not talk. His mother was a meth addict who had taken care of all of his physical needs like food, bathing and clothing, but he had spent all day every day strapped in a car seat while his mother was getting high. She never talked to him and so he never learned how to talk.

_____

_____

_____

_____

_____

☐ Not having expectations of going to school. If mom or dad didn't care if you got up for school or not. This is a form of mental abuse.

_____

_____

_____

_____

_____

☐ Not having access to age appropriate toys and books is another form of mental abuse.

_____

_____

_____

_____

_____

❏ Being placed at the "stupid table" in school is both emotional and mental abuse.

_____

_____

_____

_____

_____

❏ Being subjected to lies about yourself is mental abuse. Constantly being told you are stupid when you are smart is an example of this. One genius woman even did this to herself; she used all of her genius power to convince herself she was dumb. This is an ironic example of mental abuse of self.

_____

_____

_____

_____

_____

Emotional Abuse

❏ Most people reading this book have experienced some type of emotional abuse, or have been brought up in a family that did not teach emotional identification and expression. Our culture, our media and our schools do not teach us to talk about our feelings.

If we did know how to identify our feelings and have a safe place to process them, we would not have resentments. Therefore, in the most general sense, emotional abuse happens when we were not taught how to identify our feelings and we did not have a safe place to talk about them. Now let us look at some specific examples of emotional abuse.

☐ Being told that you should not feel a certain way or the opposite; that you should feel a certain way.

_____

_____

_____

_____

_____

_____

☐ Being shamed for wanting to talk about your feelings.

_____

_____

_____

_____

_____

_____

☐ Getting the message, however subtly, that we cannot or do not talk about emotions and feelings.

_____

_____

_____

_____

_____

_____

❑ Being taught that crying is a weakness. For example, when you were being spanked you heard "Don't cry or I will give you something to cry about."

_____

_____

_____

_____

_____

❑ Being taught that not showing your feelings is a sign of strength. Most all of men's sports fall into this category. Other jobs and professions where showing feelings is considered a liability: the medical field, EMT, emergency response, fire fighters, police and law enforcement, corrections, coronary work, the military, science and engineering, teaching and education especially math and sciences.

_____

_____

_____

_____

_____

❑ Being taught that some physical substance would make you feel better. For example, "Here have a cookie. It will make you feel better." This is called eating your feelings or emotional eating. You can substitute any food, drink or drug in the above quotation. "Here have a Percocet. It will make you feel better."

_____

_____

_____

_____

_____

☐ Isolating, which is not being allowed to have normal social contact is emotional abuse. This might have happened because of religion, addiction in the family, mental health problems in the family, physical deformities or illness of a family member. Poverty or differences in race can also cause isolation to happen.

_____

_____

_____

_____

_____

☐ Ignoring is emotional abuse. The popular saying here is, "Children are to be seen not heard." Another form of ignoring is a parent seeing their child in emotional distress and not addressing the situation in a safe affirming manner.

_____

_____

_____

_____

_____

☐ Corrupting is teaching racism, violence, ethnic bias, encouraging criminal activity, encouraging drug or alcohol abuse, rewarding children for drug dealing.

_____

_____

_____

_____

_____

☐ Exploiting is someone taking advantage of you so that they can make a profit. This is usually done in a mean or domineering way and you did not agree with it.

_____

_____

_____

_____

_____

_____

☐ Terrorizing: the most common example of this is when a child is watching domestic violence occur. Many young men have had difficulty-forgiving mom's boyfriend for beating her up. Homicidal rage is the prevalent resentment in this situation.

_____

_____

_____

_____

_____

☐ Raging is a form of terrorizing.

_____

_____

_____

_____

_____

_____

❑ A parent or loved one threatening to kill himself or herself is emotional abuse. One young woman remembered vividly the many times her mother would talk about wanting to kill herself. This was accompanied by several actual suicide attempts where the young woman had to call 911 to save her mother. This young woman was full of resentments and love for her mother.

_____

_____

_____

_____

_____

❑ Hurting pets is a form of terrorizing. One man shared the story of his brother chopping up his calico cat on a chopping block and then telling him, "If you mess with me again that will be you on the chopping block."

_____

_____

_____

_____

_____

❑ Witnessing someone being murdered is terrorizing. Knowing that someone is capable of killing you can be terrorizing. For example, mom is driving to pick her son up from a ski hill. Dad is in the passenger seat and they are fighting as usual. Mom pulls out a pistol and shoots dad dead. She arrives at the ski hill and her son gets in the back with his equipment. He asks why dad isn't saying anything and mom replies that they need to go to the police station when they get back to town. The forty-mile ride down the mountain is deathly quiet. When this young man entered treatment, he had many resentments for his mother and his dead father.

_____

_____

_____

_____

_____

_____

When Abe was seven, his dad beat him so badly he broke both his legs. Dad went to prison and Abe went to counseling. After 12 years in counseling Abe was still having night terrors. There was a monster beating him up in his dreams. He would wake up soaked with sweat and he could not go back to sleep for fear of the terror that awaited him. Abe was able to forgive and in nine weeks, he cured all the resentments that had terrorized him for 12 years. No more night terrors and his life got better in many other areas as well.

☐ Rejecting is another form of emotional abuse. Rejecting can be name calling, like "You're ugly, stupid, fat." It can be constant criticism such as hearing "I don't love you," "I should've had an abortion" or "I brought you into this world, I can take you out."

_____

_____

_____

_____

_____

_____

Spiritual Abuse

The most well publicized spiritual abuse seems to have been the scandal in the Catholic Church with priests molesting children. This happens in most religions and is spiritual abuse because the priest, pastor, minister, elder or deacon holds a position of spiritual power, which they are abusing. There can be many variations on this theme. For example, A 12 year old girl is walking home from school and is raped by a similar aged neighbor boy. The girl goes home and tells her mom what happened. Mom says, "We will tell your dad, he is a deacon at the church and he will know what to do." They tell dad and his response is, "Don't ever talk about this again! I am a deacon in the church and I don't want my position jeopardized." Mom and daughter decide to talk to the mother of the boy rapist and she replies, "My boy is an altar boy in the church and he would never do such a thing." The subject is never talked about again. The girl grows up and in her late twenties, has a baby. The baby tests positive for marijuana and child protective services require her to go to treatment and test clean before they will let her keep her baby. She did not want to have anything to do with a spiritual program of recovery because of her resentments. She resented her father and the church. She forgave both of them and started on a path of recovery, which included getting custody of her child.

_____

_____

_____

_____

_____

_____

_____

_____

❏ Another example of spiritual abuse is being told you are going to hell.

_____

_____

_____

_____

_____

_____

❏ Being taught that only members of this church are going to heaven is spiritual abuse.

_____

_____

_____

_____

_____

_____

❏ If you were raised by parents who portrayed themselves as being perfect, this is spiritual abuse because no one is perfect. There is a lot of judgementalism in this type of parenting.

_____

_____

_____

_____

_____

_____

☐ Choosing religion over relationship is a form of spiritual abuse. For example, Wally has flag football every Wednesday evening, but his parents choose to go to Bible study instead of attending his games. Wally did not want to work a spiritual program of recovery because of his resentments for his parents and anything religious or spiritual.

_____

_____

_____

_____

_____

_____

☐ One young man had resentments for his parents because they did not bring him to church and he had no religious or spiritual training.

_____

_____

_____

_____

_____

☐ Saying "I love you" while hitting or beating you is spiritual abuse.

_____

_____

_____

_____

_____

❏ Using shame and fear to control people is spiritual abuse. Many church services follow this pattern. First, you are condemned for breaking some rule, law or commandment. This is shame and fear. Then you are saved which is a great emotional event. This is repeated week after week, year after year. It is like being stuck in a revolving door. I am thrown out of the kingdom and then saved back in. The emotional upheaval is great, first I feel worthless and then I feel religious ecstasy. I might as well go sin this week so I can relate next Sunday.

_____

_____

_____

_____

_____

_____

_____

_____

_____

❏ Being forced or coerced to go to church is spiritual abuse.

_____

_____

_____

_____

_____

_____

_____

_____

Life Events That Can Generate Resentments

❏ Abandonment: A grown woman can't forget standing in front of her house at age 5. She is crying and waving goodbye to her daddy. She is a daddy's girl. She never sees him again. Years later, this abandonment issue is still causing her problems. She does not trust men and is fearful of losing whichever man she is with. She keeps re-feeling the loss of her daddy.

_____

_____

_____

_____

_____

❏ Neglect: A common scenario for feeling neglected is a parent, usually after a divorce, spending too much time with their new partner and not enough time with their child.

_____

_____

_____

_____

_____

❏ Other forms of neglect can be not getting enough: food, sleep, clothing, adequate shelter, safety, autonomy, self-esteem, sense of belonging, stability or love.

_____

_____

_____

_____

_____

❏ Verbal abuse can be more damaging than physical abuse. Many people have stated, "I would rather have been hit than verbally abused."

_____

_____

_____

_____

_____

❏ Divorce of one's parents can lead to holding resentments. Often the divorced parents will use the child in a power play with the other parent. Alternatively, one parent has resentments for the other and they tell the child openly about them. This is emotionally abusing the child because the child is forced to deal with adult emotions.

_____

_____

_____

_____

_____

❏ Materialism can also be used to manipulate children. Such as dad saying, "I will buy you a new four wheeler if you come and live with me." The child has to choose between his love for his mother or a new four-wheeler.

_____

_____

_____

_____

_____

☐ In some instances, the child leaves to go with dad for financial reasons and mom has nothing more to do with the child for choosing dad.

_____

_____

_____

_____

_____

_____

☐ Death of a loved one. Several young people have had great struggles identifying their resentments, especially anger, for a parent who has passed. For example, Daisy's father committed suicide when she was 10. She thought she was angry with God, but in reality, she had projected her anger for her father unto God. The next man in her life was her stepfather who was verbally abusive. She was very angry with him also. Daisy had built up a very effective defense mechanism to bury this anger. She even stated, "I am not an angry person." Her defenses fell apart when she exploded on her younger brother for some trivial mistake. She turned to alcohol to cope with her rage, which landed her in jail. Now she was motivated to work on her storehouse of anger. Do you need this kind of motivation also, or can you now look deep within for any hidden resentments?

_____

_____

_____

_____

_____

_____

❏ Someone you love commits suicide. People who use intellectualization as a defense mechanism often try to understand the suicide of a loved one by asking, "Why?" There probably is not an answer to this question that a logical mind can accept. The question that truly needs answering is; what do I truly feel about the suicide? In answering this question, a person can start the process of identifying their resentments. Which is the first step in the healing process.

_____

_____

_____

_____

_____

_____

❏ If someone you love tries to commit suicide and they did not die, you might have resentments.

_____

_____

_____

_____

_____

❏ If someone you love threatens to commit suicide, you might have resentments.

_____

_____

_____

_____

_____

☐ If you are thinking about committing suicide, talk to your therapist or call the National Suicide Prevention Lifeline at 1-800-273-8255.

_____

_____

_____

_____

_____

☐ Domestic Violence: If you have been the victim of domestic violence or are in an ongoing violent relationship, your resentments can be the emotional bondage that keep you powerless.

_____

_____

_____

_____

_____

☐ People, especially young men, who have watched their mothers get beaten up by their husbands/boyfriends, have had very entrenched resentments. Holding onto this rage is not conducive to your recovery.

_____

_____

_____

_____

_____

_____

☐ If you have been in a relationship and your partner cheated on you, you might have resentments. A common resentment in this situation is feeling betrayed.

_____

_____

_____

_____

_____

☐ If you were the one doing the cheating, you might have resentments for yourself. Read the chapter on forgiving yourself.

_____

_____

_____

_____

_____

☐ Children or teens who find out that one of their parents are having an affair can develop resentments. For example, A 12 year old boy discovers his father is having an affair. The father tells him, "Don't you dare tell your mother." This young man had resentments for his father.

_____

_____

_____

_____

_____

_____

❑ Broken First Loves: An extremely difficult group of resentments to heal is when a teenager falls in love and then their lover breaks up with them.

_____

_____

_____

_____

_____

_____

❑ Drinking with your parents can be abusive to a person who develops alcoholism. In this situation, the parents did not willfully abuse the child, but they taught their child that drinking was OK and this belief system does not work for a person with the disease of alcoholism.

_____

_____

_____

_____

_____

❑ Using drugs with a parent or parents is abusive. When we are young, our parents are our higher powers and when they teach us that drug use is OK, they are doing us a powerful wrong.

_____

_____

_____

_____

_____

☐ Another type of abuse seen in addict families is the parent making statements such as, "Why can't you just smoke pot like us? Why do you have to smoke meth?" Any other drug could be substituted for meth in this scenario.

_____

_____

_____

_____

_____

☐ Being spoiled is abusive because the person is taught to have expectations without having to work for them. Addiction thrives in this environment!

_____

_____

_____

_____

_____

☐ Being enabled is different from being spoiled in that there is a safety net to catch the person before they hit their bottom and so things never get bad enough for them to stop irresponsible behaviors. Examples have included a rich grandma who was always there with her checkbook to bail out her grandson who kept being jailed due to his drug problems. Another all too common example is a parent paying the rent and bills of their child which enables the child to spend whatever money they have on drinking and drugging.

_____

_____

_____

_____

_____

❏ If you have been diagnosed with PTSD, you probably have resentments.

_____

_____

_____

_____

_____

❏ If you have been traumatized, you probably have resentments.

_____

_____

_____

_____

_____

❏ War and conflict often generate resentments.

_____

_____

_____

_____

_____

❏ If you were adopted, you can have deeply buried resentments of worthlessness and abandonment.

_____

_____

_____

_____

_____

Use the following space to write about any resentments that you may have which were not covered in the previous pages. Your memories might have been triggered and now is a good time and place to put them down on paper.

_____

_____

_____

_____

_____

_____

_____

_____

_____

_____

_____

_____

_____

_____

_____

_____

_____

_____

_____

_____

IDENTIFYING
YOUR RESENTMENTS

Now that you have read the previous pages about where resentments come from, you are ready to move on and put down on paper (using a feeling list) your resentments. Use one of the feelings list located on the following pages. Tear out one of the feelings lists. On the top, write the name of the person you are working on. Go through the list of feelings and circle the ones you hold against this person. Refer back to the life situations you have checked or highlighted to help identify your resentments. Only do this for one person at a time. It is not unusual to have 40 to 70 feelings circled.

If you do not know the name of the person who abused you, you can use a general term like rapist. It does not have to be a person who abused you. It could be an organization like the government, Wall Street, the army, etc. It could also be something such as cancer as one young woman had many resentments for the cancer that was killing her mother. Some people have had resentments for God and have used this process successfully on this issue.

Narrowing down the feelings circled.

Next, we need to narrow down the circled feelings to approximately 10 to 15. We do not have to forgive a person for every resentment because forgiveness is generalizable, which means that if we forgive the big resentments, it will take care of the smaller ones also. So, go through your list of circled feelings and put a star or check mark next to the big ones. The ones that have a lot of emotional energy in them. If you have circled the feelings of hopeless, helpless and worthless, put a check or star next to them because these are the suicide emotions. It does not matter if you have active suicidal thoughts or not, you might still have been committing suicide on the installment plan by slowly drinking or drugging yourself to death. These three feelings are usually the cause of such behavior and need to be healed.

FEELINGS LIST

Abandoned	Contemptuous	Godforsaken	Needy	Shy	Unforgivable
Abused	Complacent	Gross	Neglected	Sick	Unhappy
Afraid	Corrupted	Guilty	Nervous	Smothered	Unimportant
Agitated	Crazy	Hateful	Oppositional	Smug	Unlovable
Agony	Crippled	Heartache	Overwhelmed	Sorrowful	Unloved
Alienated	Cynical	Heart-broken	Pain	Spoiled	Unmanageable
Angry	Deceived	Helpless	Pessimistic	Stereotyped	Unprotected
Annoyed	Defeated	Homicidal Rage	Powerless	Stressed-out	Unsure
Anxious	Defiant	Hopeless	Prideful	Stuck	Untouchable
Apathetic	Degraded	Horrified	Privileged	Stuck-up	Upset
Arrogant	Depressed	Humiliated	Provoked	Stupid	Used
Awkward	Devalued	Hurt	Rage	Submissive	Useless
Attacked	Dirty	Ignored	Regretful	Suicidal	Vengeful
Bankrupt	Disappointed	Insignificant	Rejected	Suspicious	Violated
Betrayed	Discouraged	Intimidated	Sad	Tense	Vulnerable
Bitter	Disgusted	Isolated	Scared	Terrified	Wasted
Bored	Distrustful	Judged	Selfish	Terrorized	Weak
Brain Washed	Disturbed	Lonely	Self-absorbed	Threatened	Worn-out
Bullied	Empty	Mad	Self-centered	Torn-up	Worried
Burdened	Entitled	Miserable	Self-conscious	Tormented	Worthless
Cheated	Exhausted	Misguided	Self-pity	Trapped	Worth-less
Conceited	Exploited	Mislead	Self-righteous	Traumatized	Wretched
Condemned	Fearful	Misunderstood	Sexualized	Troubled	
Conflicted	Frustrated	Mixed-up	Shame	Ugly	
Confused	Gloomy	Nauseous	Shocked	Uncomfortable	

FEELINGS LIST

Abandoned	Contemptuous	Godforsaken	Needy	Shy	Unforgivable
Abused	Complacent	Gross	Neglected	Sick	Unhappy
Afraid	Corrupted	Guilty	Nervous	Smothered	Unimportant
Agitated	Crazy	Hateful	Oppositional	Smug	Unlovable
Agony	Crippled	Heartache	Overwhelmed	Sorrowful	Unloved
Alienated	Cynical	Heart-broken	Pain	Spoiled	Unmanageable
Angry	Deceived	Helpless	Pessimistic	Stereotyped	Unprotected
Annoyed	Defeated	Homicidal Rage	Powerless	Stressed-out	Unsure
Anxious	Defiant	Hopeless	Prideful	Stuck	Untouchable
Apathetic	Degraded	Horrified	Privileged	Stuck-up	Upset
Arrogant	Depressed	Humiliated	Provoked	Stupid	Used
Awkward	Devalued	Hurt	Rage	Submissive	Useless
Attacked	Dirty	Ignored	Regretful	Suicidal	Vengeful
Bankrupt	Disappointed	Insignificant	Rejected	Suspicious	Violated
Betrayed	Discouraged	Intimidated	Sad	Tense	Vulnerable
Bitter	Disgusted	Isolated	Scared	Terrified	Wasted
Bored	Distrustful	Judged	Selfish	Terrorized	Weak
Brain Washed	Disturbed	Lonely	Self-absorbed	Threatened	Worn-out
Bullied	Empty	Mad	Self-centered	Torn-up	Worried
Burdened	Entitled	Miserable	Self-conscious	Tormented	Worthless
Cheated	Exhausted	Misguided	Self-pity	Trapped	Worth-less
Conceited	Exploited	Mislead	Self-righteous	Traumatized	Wretched
Condemned	Fearful	Misunderstood	Sexualized	Troubled	
Conflicted	Frustrated	Mixed-up	Shame	Ugly	
Confused	Gloomy	Nauseous	Shocked	Uncomfortable	

FEELINGS LIST

Abandoned	Contemptuous	Godforsaken	Needy	Shy	Unforgivable
Abused	Complacent	Gross	Neglected	Sick	Unhappy
Afraid	Corrupted	Guilty	Nervous	Smothered	Unimportant
Agitated	Crazy	Hateful	Oppositional	Smug	Unlovable
Agony	Crippled	Heartache	Overwhelmed	Sorrowful	Unloved
Alienated	Cynical	Heart-broken	Pain	Spoiled	Unmanageable
Angry	Deceived	Helpless	Pessimistic	Stereotyped	Unprotected
Annoyed	Defeated	Homicidal Rage	Powerless	Stressed-out	Unsure
Anxious	Defiant	Hopeless	Prideful	Stuck	Untouchable
Apathetic	Degraded	Horrified	Privileged	Stuck-up	Upset
Arrogant	Depressed	Humiliated	Provoked	Stupid	Used
Awkward	Devalued	Hurt	Rage	Submissive	Useless
Attacked	Dirty	Ignored	Regretful	Suicidal	Vengeful
Bankrupt	Disappointed	Insignificant	Rejected	Suspicious	Violated
Betrayed	Discouraged	Intimidated	Sad	Tense	Vulnerable
Bitter	Disgusted	Isolated	Scared	Terrified	Wasted
Bored	Distrustful	Judged	Selfish	Terrorized	Weak
Brain Washed	Disturbed	Lonely	Self-absorbed	Threatened	Worn-out
Bullied	Empty	Mad	Self-centered	Torn-up	Worried
Burdened	Entitled	Miserable	Self-conscious	Tormented	Worthless
Cheated	Exhausted	Misguided	Self-pity	Trapped	Worth-less
Conceited	Exploited	Mislead	Self-righteous	Traumatized	Wretched
Condemned	Fearful	Misunderstood	Sexualized	Troubled	
Conflicted	Frustrated	Mixed-up	Shame	Ugly	
Confused	Gloomy	Nauseous	Shocked	Uncomfortable	

FEELINGS LIST

Abandoned	Contemptuous	Godforsaken	Needy	Shy	Unforgivable
Abused	Complacent	Gross	Neglected	Sick	Unhappy
Afraid	Corrupted	Guilty	Nervous	Smothered	Unimportant
Agitated	Crazy	Hateful	Oppositional	Smug	Unlovable
Agony	Crippled	Heartache	Overwhelmed	Sorrowful	Unloved
Alienated	Cynical	Heart-broken	Pain	Spoiled	Unmanageable
Angry	Deceived	Helpless	Pessimistic	Stereotyped	Unprotected
Annoyed	Defeated	Homicidal Rage	Powerless	Stressed-out	Unsure
Anxious	Defiant	Hopeless	Prideful	Stuck	Untouchable
Apathetic	Degraded	Horrified	Privileged	Stuck-up	Upset
Arrogant	Depressed	Humiliated	Provoked	Stupid	Used
Awkward	Devalued	Hurt	Rage	Submissive	Useless
Attacked	Dirty	Ignored	Regretful	Suicidal	Vengeful
Bankrupt	Disappointed	Insignificant	Rejected	Suspicious	Violated
Betrayed	Discouraged	Intimidated	Sad	Tense	Vulnerable
Bitter	Disgusted	Isolated	Scared	Terrified	Wasted
Bored	Distrustful	Judged	Selfish	Terrorized	Weak
Brain Washed	Disturbed	Lonely	Self-absorbed	Threatened	Worn-out
Bullied	Empty	Mad	Self-centered	Torn-up	Worried
Burdened	Entitled	Miserable	Self-conscious	Tormented	Worthless
Cheated	Exhausted	Misguided	Self-pity	Trapped	Worth-less
Conceited	Exploited	Mislead	Self-righteous	Traumatized	Wretched
Condemned	Fearful	Misunderstood	Sexualized	Troubled	
Conflicted	Frustrated	Mixed-up	Shame	Ugly	
Confused	Gloomy	Nauseous	Shocked	Uncomfortable	

FEELINGS LIST

Abandoned	Contemptuous	Godforsaken	Needy	Shy	Unforgivable
Abused	Complacent	Gross	Neglected	Sick	Unhappy
Afraid	Corrupted	Guilty	Nervous	Smothered	Unimportant
Agitated	Crazy	Hateful	Oppositional	Smug	Unlovable
Agony	Crippled	Heartache	Overwhelmed	Sorrowful	Unloved
Alienated	Cynical	Heart-broken	Pain	Spoiled	Unmanageable
Angry	Deceived	Helpless	Pessimistic	Stereotyped	Unprotected
Annoyed	Defeated	Homicidal Rage	Powerless	Stressed-out	Unsure
Anxious	Defiant	Hopeless	Prideful	Stuck	Untouchable
Apathetic	Degraded	Horrified	Privileged	Stuck-up	Upset
Arrogant	Depressed	Humiliated	Provoked	Stupid	Used
Awkward	Devalued	Hurt	Rage	Submissive	Useless
Attacked	Dirty	Ignored	Regretful	Suicidal	Vengeful
Bankrupt	Disappointed	Insignificant	Rejected	Suspicious	Violated
Betrayed	Discouraged	Intimidated	Sad	Tense	Vulnerable
Bitter	Disgusted	Isolated	Scared	Terrified	Wasted
Bored	Distrustful	Judged	Selfish	Terrorized	Weak
Brain Washed	Disturbed	Lonely	Self-absorbed	Threatened	Worn-out
Bullied	Empty	Mad	Self-centered	Torn-up	Worried
Burdened	Entitled	Miserable	Self-conscious	Tormented	Worthless
Cheated	Exhausted	Misguided	Self-pity	Trapped	Worth-less
Conceited	Exploited	Mislead	Self-righteous	Traumatized	Wretched
Condemned	Fearful	Misunderstood	Sexualized	Troubled	
Conflicted	Frustrated	Mixed-up	Shame	Ugly	
Confused	Gloomy	Nauseous	Shocked	Uncomfortable	

FILLING OUT
THE PRAYER FORMAT

Take one of the prayer formats found on the following pages and follow the example below to fill it out.

_____Mom_____ I forgive you for causing me to feel _abandoned,_
(name of person)

afraid, betrayed, confused, defiant,

fearful, hopeless, hurt, lonely, unloved

and worthless.

_____God_____ I ask you to forgive ___my mom___ also.
(name of Higher Power)   (name)

_____ I forgive you for causing me to feel _____
       (name of person)

_____

_____

_____

_____

_____ I ask you to forgive _____ also.
    (name of Higher Power)   (name)

_____ I forgive you for causing me to feel _____
(name of person)

_____

_____

_____

_____

_____ I ask you to forgive _____ also.
(name of Higher Power)   (name)

_____ I forgive you for causing me to feel _____

      (name of person)

_____

_____

_____

_____

_____ I ask you to forgive _____ also.

     (name of Higher Power)   (name)

_____ I forgive you for causing me to feel _____
(name of person)

_____

_____

_____

_____ I ask you to forgive _____ also.
(name of Higher Power)   (name)

_____ I forgive you for causing me to feel _____
(name of person)

_____

_____

_____

_____

_____ I ask you to forgive _____ also.
(name of Higher Power)   (name)

HEALING INSTRUCTIONS

To forgive the person, simply say this prayer out loud two times per day. If you want to heal faster, say it more often. The following story is an example of a girl who healed her resentments in one night.

We will call her the Tiger because she was cold and unfeeling. She had stood before the same judge eight times and had never shown any emotion, just her cold unfeeling stare. For a 19 year old, she had many probation violations for smoking marijuana and domestic violence. She had broken her stepfather's nose on two occasions. In her last sentencing, the judge had told her that since she was turning 18, her next probation violation would result in a 90 sentence to the county jail. The Tiger was participating in outpatient counseling and didn't violate her probation for over a year. She was offered Forgiveness Therapy on several occasions to heal her resentments for her deceased father but had declined. Some friends showed up at the Tiger's house and they were smoking weed. It was offered to her and being a powerless addict, she smoked it. The next day, she had a probation visit and was drug tested. She tested positive for marijuana and was immediately put in jail. At her preliminary hearing, she asked the judge for a furlough and explained that she needed to go to a counseling session to write a forgiveness prayer to her father that she had been putting off for a year. She was given the furlough and came in for a counseling session. She finally wrote the forgiveness prayer to her father that she had been putting off. The Tiger took the prayer back to jail with her and stayed up all night repeating it. She stated in a later session, "I said it 50,000 times that night." The next day was her sentencing. When asked for her statement, she tearfully explained her situation to the judge. The Tiger had cried! The judge was moved by her tears and had a change of heart. He did not sentence her to the threatened 90 days in jail. He let her out on probation and she was able to graduate from high school with her class. She also quit smoking pot for good. The Tiger had healed her resentments in one night of saying her forgiveness prayer!

Some people have even healed their resentments with one saying of the prayer. Charley is a good example. He got into recovery 25 years ago, but could not get more than a few months clean and sober before relapsing. This happened again and again for 25 years. He went to the best rehabs that money could buy, but still he continued to relapse. The reason for this was that he had a resentment for his father that he refused to talk about with anybody, until he was shown Forgiveness Therapy. Charley circled his resentments on a feelings list, narrowed them down to the biggest ones and then composed a forgiveness prayer. He said the prayer out loud and then stated with an elated look on his face, "I finally got it!" Got what? "That light feeling I heard so many people talk about in rehab. I feel like I am floating six inches off this chair!" Charley has been clean and sober for 7 years since saying the prayer one time. There are no guarantees that this will happen to you, but it could.

THE FORGIVENESS TEST

When are we done with resentments for a person? The simple answer is when we can pass the Forgiveness Test. Here is how you take the Forgiveness Test.

1. Sit on a chair with both feet flat on the floor.

2. Place your right hand on your heart.

3. Close your eyes.

4. Repeat the first line of the Forgiveness Prayer. For example, Mom I forgive you for causing me to feel _____

    _____

    _____

    _____.

5. Feel with your right hand what resentment is left in your heart for this person and say it out loud.

6. Repeat this process three times.

Now continuing with the example,

Mom I forgive you for causing me to feel <u>sad</u>.

Mom I forgive you for causing me to feel <u>free</u>.

Mom I forgive you for causing me to feel <u>peaceful</u>.

Will feeling sad, free and peaceful cause me to relapse into drinking or drug use? No. The test is passed and the resentments are healed.

If there are still uncomfortable resentments left in your heart, continue saying the Forgiveness Prayer, but change the feelings to reflect what resentments are still present.

When you can pass the Forgiveness Test, you are done with that person. Now you can move on to forgiving the next person you hold resentments against. Continue with the process until you have no more resentments. You really can be happy, joyous and free!

The Forgiveness Test requires you to be honest with yourself. To thine own self be true. This is where rigorous honesty is crucial to your recovery. If you lie to yourself about your resentments, you are disrespecting yourself. In addition, you are denying the reality of your feelings/resentments and this will keep you sick.

WILLINGNESS

A 16-year-old Hispanic girl is beaten up by her father and he goes to jail. Then, she is sexually molested by her 18-year-old cousin. She readily forgives her father, but is unwilling to forgive her cousin. She comes up with a great idea and states, "I am going to ask God for the willingness to forgive my cousin." After three days of asking God for the willingness to forgive her cousin, she gets it. She writes the prayer, repeats it daily until she has forgiven her cousin. What a great idea. Thanks for sharing.

If you don't have the willingness to forgive, you can learn from this 16-year-old girl and ask your higher power for it. Your asking can be a simple prayer like; God, I ask you for the willingness to forgive _____

_____

_____

_____

_____

_____

_____.

SPIRITUAL EXPERIENCES

A small percentage of people who have started saying forgiveness prayers have had spiritual experiences. These experiences are usually so far out of the realm of normal experiencing that people rarely have the words to describe them. For that reason, we will mention three of the most common types so that if they happen to you, you can use them to help you stay clean and sober and not be filled with irrational fear about the experience. Do not go to a psychologist or psychiatrist to try to understand these types of experiences. They do not have the appropriate training. They might even give you a diagnosis of paranoid schizophrenia. Moreover, if you believe their diagnosis, then you have minimized one of the best gifts of the spirit.

White Light Experiences

People who have seen the white light usually have similar descriptions such as; the most beautiful white light they have ever seen, very easy on the eyes, very loving, if love were visible it would look like this, I was drawn toward it and wanted to stay with it forever, a great sense of peace enveloped me.

If you have a white light experience and want to learn more about it, many books describe what people have experienced. These books can help you to incorporate this experience into your recovery. White light experiences are often life changing experiences. A true story of a white light experience that changed a woman's life is told below.

The Story of Deedee

Deedee was a chronic alcoholic. She had been in and out of alcoholic treatment and psyche wards numerous times in her adult life. Through her substantial counseling, Deedee had gained much awareness, admittance and acceptance of her resentments, yet she continued to hold on to major resentments against her father and her ex-husband. Deedee agreed to try forgiveness Therapy and wrote a letter to her dad identifying her resentments. She then wrote a prayer forgiving him. She repeated the prayer daily until testing revealed that she had forgiven her father. She started to remember some positive and tender moments that they had shared when she was a child.

Deedee was struggling mightily with her resentments towards her ex-husband. She would clench her fists in session and exclaim that she would never let go of these resentments. Tapping into this storehouse of pain and hurt was overwhelming and she would often resort to her old behavior of drinking to cope with this pain. She even tried to commit suicide to cope with her feelings. Another side of Deedee wanted to be free of these resentments and would cry for some relief from the pain of her internal struggle. Deedee said her forgiveness prayer to her ex-husband sporadically and not much was changing. Deedee came in for a session and was strangely silent. When asked if everything was all right, Deedee said she was afraid to talk about an experience she had because she thought she would be judged crazy. When she was reassured that this would not happen and she would not be put into a psyche ward again, Deedee related the following experience but struggled to find the words to describe it. She said that she was home alone and had not been drinking. She was meditating and something happened. Deedee stated that her house was filled with the most beautiful white light and she knew it was God. She stated that she was in presence of God for three hours. She said that during this time, she cried out all the hurt and pain she had been carrying inside for so long. Deedee said that it was the most wondrous experience that she had ever had. She had never before experienced such Love, acceptance and joy. She finally let out all of the tears and pain that she had been holding in for decades and decades.

Deedee had several characteristics of a person who has had a white light experience. She feared being judged as crazy, she had a hard time finding descriptor words and she had experienced joy. This experience was the turning point in her recovery and had it been discounted in any way, she might not have been able to use it to change her life for the positive.

Epiphany

An epiphany is when a person has a sudden realization of some great spiritual fact or idea. Some people, who have been saying forgiveness prayers, have had an epiphany. The story of White Cloud is an example of a person who had an epiphany.

White Cloud was a 19-year-old Native American who had two big resentments. The first was for a past girlfriend who had hurt him deeply and the second was for his brothers who would sexually abuse him when they were all high on cocaine. White Cloud forgave his girlfriend and was almost finished forgiving his brothers when he had a vision. In this vision, he saw what his future purpose in life was meant to be. He saw himself as a Native American Christian healer who would go from reservation to reservation helping other Native Americans to heal from their drug use, alcoholism and sexual abuse issues. He was keenly aware that Natives did not like to talk about these issues, but he was inspired by his vision to start talking about it with other Native Americans. He was going to share his experience, strength and hope to help others heal. Prior to this epiphany, White Cloud had no idea what he was going to do with his life. He had no purpose. His epiphany gave him a purpose.

Quantum Change Experience

A quantum change experience is when a person experiences a large amount of change is a short amount of time. Some people who have been doing forgiveness prayers have had quantum change experiences. A good example would be Angela.

Angela was raised by parents who were swingers and heroin addicts. Therefore, Angela became a swinger and a heroin addict as well. Angela fell in love with a man who did not like her lifestyle, so Angela entered rehab. She was working on her resentments and was struggling, as many people do, with admitting that her parents had abused her by teaching her the swinging, heroin addict lifestyle. Angela had composed a forgiveness prayer to her parents but could not bring herself to say it out loud. Her struggle was causing her to feel irritable, annoyed, aggravated, frustrated and confused. Her mood was affecting all of the other women in the house, and not in a good way. Angela decided to take a shower to try to calm down. While she was taking the shower, she decided to say her forgiveness prayer out loud. Something transformational happened to her. The next day, Angela was the talk of rehab. All of the women in the house took notice of the change in Angela. One of them stated, "Before she went into the shower, she was a bitch. But when she came out, it was like she was a completely new person. Like an angel. She was so peaceful and calm." When Angela was asked "What happened?" She responded, "I was feeling really irritated, confused and frustrated, so I decided to take a shower to calm down. In the shower, I decided to say my forgiveness prayer to my parents out loud for the first time. Then I saw my whole life flash before my eyes. I saw all the swinger parties, all the naked bodies having sex in our pool, the people shooting up heroin in the open and not trying to hide it, and my parents were a part of it all. They encouraged me to join in. Then I saw my future as a blank slate and I could fill it in with whatever images I wanted to. I didn't need to repeat the images of my past." In her quantum change experience, Angela found great peace and hope for her future with the love of her life, her boyfriend.

HOW TO FORGIVE YOURSELF

Forgiving yourself can be as important as forgiving others. What follows are six ideas to help you to forgive yourself. These were developed from a decade of teaching people how to forgive.

1. **Change your behaviors.** You can behave your way into forgiving yourself by changing your behaviors that cause you to feel guilty and ashamed. The religious word for this is repentance, which means to turn from you evil ways and turn to good ways of behaving. Many religions teach repentance and forgiveness together, but some people have confused having a feeling of repentance with changing one's behaviors. Changing the behaviors is the required action to forgiving yourself.

2. **When doing Step 2 of the 12 Steps of AA or NA, get a forgiving higher power.** Some of us were raised with a judging, condemning God and while this can be a character trait of a higher power, if it is not balanced out with character traits of forgiving, loving and caring, a person will struggle with forgiving themselves.

3. **Making amends to those you have hurt will help you to forgive yourself.** This is the work of Steps 8 and 9 of the 12 Step Program, which provides clear instructions on how to make amends. You can also make amends to yourself.

4. **Change your thinking.** If you cannot say, "I forgive myself," then you have a thinking error. You can change your thinking by repeating, "I forgive myself." Your addiction does not want you to forgive yourself. It only wants to condemn you as worthless and then why not get drunk or high?

5. **Forgive others.** You can make progress on forgiving yourself by forgiving others. If you believe in the spiritual principle found in the Lord's Prayer which states, "And forgive us our trespasses as we forgive those who have trespassed against us." This principle states that God will only forgive you as much as you forgive others. And how can you forgive yourself more than God forgives you? So, if you want to know that you are completely forgiven, then completely forgive those who have hurt you. In other words, get rid of all your resentments by forgiving.

6. **Go to 12 Step meetings.** At these meetings, you will hear people who do not regret the past nor wish to shut the door on it. They can do this because they have forgiven themselves and those who have hurt them. You can learn from their examples. For example, a man in a 12 Step meeting shared that he had accidentally killed his brother when they were teenagers. This man talked openly about the accident without any self-condemnation because he had forgiven himself. If this man can do it, then surely I can learn to forgive myself.

WHY FORGIVENESS AND NOT SOME OTHER TYPES OF THERAPY?

The simple answer is because it is faster and possibly more effective than other types of therapy. We will return to Abe's story as an example.

Abe was 7 years old when his father broke both of his legs in a fit of rage. Dad went to prison for it. Mom divorced dad, moved away and remarried. Abe went to therapy. After 12 years of therapy, Abe was still terrorized by a demon in his sleep. He never knew a full night's sleep because he would wake up from his terrorizing nightmares with his sheets soaking wet from his sweats. He could not go back to sleep for fear of the demon of his dreams, his father. Abe had rage problems, anxiety problems, alcohol and drug use problems, school problems, relationship problems and finally legal problems. He was charged with attempted manslaughter when he and two friends tried to kick another young man to death.

Abe was asked if during all of his prior 12 years of therapy the idea of forgiveness was ever presented to him as a way to heal. He stated, "No, but one therapist suggested that he do needle point to help with his rage and anxiety!" Abe was asked if he would like to try Forgiveness Therapy as a way to heal his resentments towards his father. He said that he would try and after nine weeks of doing forgiveness work on his father, all of Abe's symptoms went away. No more terrorizing nightmares. No more anxiety from fear and lack of sleep. Improved grades. Better relationships. No more drug and alcohol use. No more rage! In 9 weeks of doing Forgiveness Therapy, he had accomplished what he had not been able to do in 12 years of therapy!

Ted's Story

Ted was beaten regularly by his parents from an early age. He developed oppositional defiance disorder, alcoholism and drug addiction. Ted got clean and sober and spent three years in therapy including EMDR (Eye Movement Desensitization and Reprocessing), but he was still full of anger and rage. A true dry drunk. It was not until Ted learned how to forgive his parents and actually did the work of forgiving, that he could experience the peace, joy and happiness that his recovering brothers and sisters were talking about.

Then a tragedy happened in Ted's life. His wife of 31 years left him for another man. This life situation was going to be a real test of his recovery skills. Ted's children feared that he would return to alcohol to cope, but he did not. He turned to forgiveness. He used the method presented in this book to forgive his ex-wife and was again able to feel happy, joyous and free. It did not happen overnight as Ted is slow to forgive, but with 2½ years of saying forgiveness prayers, he is now grateful for the marriage. Which is a whole lot better than being filled with resentments and drunk.

Can forgiveness really be that effective? Doubting can be a normal part of your process when first presented with the evidence about how fast Forgiveness Therapy can work. Many people, who were doubters and had tried other types of therapy without success, were willing to try forgiveness and found healing. Remember the acronym HOW. HOW do we recover? By being Honest, Open and Willing. Are you willing to try to heal with Forgiveness Therapy? If on the other hand, you remain doubtful and have contempt prior to investigation, you will retain your resentments and probably relapse.

FORGIVENESS, A TOOL FOR EVERYDAY LIVING

Forgiveness is not only an excellent tool for healing past resentments, but it can be used to calm upsetting emotions as they are happening in the present. For example.

Bob is late for work and speeding down the interstate. Up ahead, a semi-truck moves into the left lane to pass another slow moving semi. Bob races up behind the semi in the left lane and catches a case of road rage. He starts cursing out the semi driver. Bob's emotions are out of control, but he remembers his recovery tool of forgiveness. Bob states aloud, "Semi truck driver, I forgive you for causing me to feel rage and frustration. God I ask you to forgive the semi-truck driver also." This simple statement settles Bob's emotions and he arrives at work in a much-improved emotional state.

Another example: Tammi walks out of the rehab clinical director's office and starts to curse out the director for recommending that she take an extension. A peer asks Tammi to say a forgiveness prayer by repeating after her and Tammi agrees. Together they say out loud, "Clinical director, I forgive you for causing me to feel angry, judgmental, impulsive and frustrated. God I ask you to forgive the clinical director also." Tammi's emotions subside and she is able to see the logic behind the clinical director's recommendation.

Forgiveness is a simple tool to help settle high emotions. If a person is making decisions based on these high emotions, they are entering into addictive thinking and losing touch with rational thought. Using forgiveness will help keep you in a spiritual program of recovery.

PICKING THEM UP AGAIN

Once a person obtains freedom from their resentments, it is possible to pick them up again. There can be reminders of old situations that trigger feelings of resentment. Usually these feelings have a lot less energy than the original ones, but they can still be troublesome. If a person starts to obsess about them by attaching thoughts to them, they start to grow and take on a life of their own. You can stop this process by saying a forgiveness prayer, which has the troublesome emotions in it.

For example, Ted, whose story is related earlier in this book, is watching a movie where a wife is cheating on her husband. He is triggered to feel cheated, betrayed, angry, unloved and rejected. He goes to bed with these feelings and dreams about his wife cheating on him. The next morning, he wakes up in a bad mood because he has picked up his old resentments. He needs a quick way to relieve himself of these feelings. Ted recites a simple forgiveness prayer to his ex-wife, "Ex-wife I forgive you for causing me to feel cheated, betrayed, angry, unloved and rejected. God, I ask you to forgive my ex-wife also." Now, Ted can smile at himself in the mirror when he is shaving because he has freed himself from those ugly resentments. Today, he can feel happy, joyous and free.

Feelings are emotional energy that flows through us. If we dam up the flow of our feeling energy by hanging on to it, we are creating resentments. Forgiveness clears the way for the feelings to flow on without being dammed up.

KNOWLEDGE OR WISDOM

The knowledge in this book is just that, knowledge. In order for this knowledge to change your life, you need to put it to work. Which means, do not just read the book, do the work. Identify your resentments, narrow them down to the big ones, write the forgiveness prayer and repeat it at least twice daily until your resentments are gone. Then the knowledge has become wisdom. You are worth it and anything of worth takes work. Peace, joy and happiness is waiting for you at the end of the work.

THE BEST WAY OF FORGIVENESS

The best way for forgiveness to happen is for the person who has done the hurting to admit to the one they hurt what they have done and then ask for forgiveness. If in reading this book, you have realized that you have hurt someone with your words or actions and you would like to make amends, go to the person, tell them how you have hurt them and ask them to forgive you. That is all you can do unless you owe them money or some other materialistic thing. You cannot force them to forgive you. You can only ask for forgiveness. The rest is on them.

Resentments and forgiveness workbooks are available on *Amazon.com*. Also available is "Opening The Door To Freedom With Forgiveness Therapy" by Wayne Kauppila.